# LOVE VEGAN

## The Essential Indian Cookbook for Vegans

Zoe Hazan

 HIGH CEDAR PRESS

# LOVE VEGAN

## The Essential Indian Cookbook for Vegans

High Cedar Press

Copyright © 2017

Paperback Edition

Published by High Cedar Press

Illustrations Copyright © 2017

# DISCLAIMER

The full contents of 'Love Vegan', including text, comments, graphics, images, and other content are for informational purposes only. The information is not intended to diagnose, treat, cure or prevent any illnesses or diseases. Always consult you physician before changing dietary habits.

'Love Vegan' does not provide specific information or advice regarding food intolerance or allergies. It is the responsibility of the reader to ensure any diagnosed or potential food intolerances are identified and excluded from the recipes.

The author and publisher make no guarantee as to the availability of ingredients mentioned in this book. Many ingredients vary in size and texture and these differences may affect the outcome of some recipes. The author has tried to make the recipes as accurate and workable as possible, however, cannot be responsible for any recipe not working.

Every effort has been made to prepare this material to ensure it's accuracy, however, the author nor publisher will be held responsible if there is information deemed as inaccurate.

# CONTENTS

• • • • • • • • • • • • • • • • • • • • • • • • • • •

## MAINS

# CONTENTS

• • • • • • • • • • • • • • • • • • • • • • • •

## SIDES

## INDIAN SWEETS

## CHUTNEYS

# INTRODUCTION

Indian cuisine is universally known for its flavorsome and lively dishes. In the West, Indian food has become so popular that curry is often referred to as the British national dish. The richness of Indian cuisine lies in its diversity and this cookbook opens up a whole world of authentic Indian dishes to vegans.

Celebrate the rich and exciting diversity of Indian food, whether you're a creamy korma fan or a full-on chili fiend, Love vegan has the perfect recipe for you. Prepare yourself for a world of recipes that are full of spices, rich aromas, and aromatic flavors - all cooked with ease within your very own kitchen.

From Goan Vindaloo Tofu and Creamy Vegan Butter 'Chicken' to Spiced Potato and Pea Parathas and Crispy Zucchini Bhajis, this cookbook focuses on the lively flavors of India and shows you how easy it is to prepare exotic and delicious vegan dishes in your very own kitchen - on even the busiest of weeknights.

'Love Vegan: The Essential Indian Cookbook for Vegans' features all the delicious recipes you'll ever need for a real Indian experience, which can be prepared in less than 30 minutes, using simple and easy to follow instructions suitable for even the most inexperienced cook.

This cookbook offers recipes which are made with easy to source ingredients, so not only you will spend little time preparing, but you will not have to run around looking for hard to find speciality items.

This cookbook series aims to shed some light on the vegan lifestyle and health benefits that will follow. We believe that whatever your reasons are for integrating vegan food into your diet the end result should be full of flavor and authenticity. Whether you are a vegan, a vegetarian or a meat-eater looking to reduce the amount of meat based meals in your diet this book can help inspire you to cook delicious meals every night of the week.

So what are you waiting for, start your Indian vegan journey today!

# VEGANISM

The vegetarian revolution is a culinary movement that has truly gathered steam over the past few years. According to a recent report, 1 in 8 UK adults now follow either a vegetarian or vegan diet and this number reaches 1 in 5 for those between the ages of 16-24.

Whether you want to seek ways to optimize your own health and well-being, or whether you are concerned about reducing animal suffering and the environment - being part of the vegan movement is definitely the path to follow.

Veganism is a stricter form of vegetarianism. For many vegetarians it's also the next step. Whether a vegan or vegetarian, The Love Vegan series is here to help you with quick and easy recipes to prepare. We have done the research for you and have put together this essential Indian cookbook that proves you can still enjoy your favorite dishes while following a vegan lifestyle.

# HOW TO INTEGRATE VEGANISM INTO YOUR LIFE

Vegans eat foods which only come from a plant-based sources. Western cultures rely heavily on meat and fish, so it is perfectly fine if you wish to transition slowly as you may need time to adjust to a new way of living. The transition from being a meat-eater to a vegan needs to be slow and well planned in order for it to be successful.

First and foremost, you need to make sure that you understand the basic nutritional facts about vegan ingredients. Proportions and size of servings are important for you to thrive on a vegan diet and you will need to plan your meals and snacks carefully.

You can bring health and compassion to your table without being a full time vegan. Many cultures have adopted a part-time vegan lifestyle.

In India, where animal based products are consumed far less than in the Western world, it's not uncommon to have a certain number of days in a week or even months in a year when a vegan diet rules.

Veganism doesn't mean that you have to eat leaves and lettuce all day or miss out on your favorite foods. It is very important to learn the nutritional value of ingredients and to plan varied meals throughout the day. Your body will let you know quickly enough if it doesn't get the necessary nutrients.

# WHAT CAN YOU EAT?

If it had a face, eyes, fins, feet or wings, ban it from your plate! If it's sourced from a plant, go for it. It gets a little more involved and less straightforward with by-products.

For example, can you eat honey? The answer is no, as it's an animal by-product.

Another example would be the 'Gelatin Conundrum'. Used mostly to bind and thicken, gelatin is obtained by boiling animal parts, therefore for a long time it was not suitable for vegan diets but, it's now possible to find vegetable based gelatin made from soy and seaweeds. Look for the international vegan trademark which is found on vegan-friendly products, as well as ingredients which have been highlighted as an allergen such as eggs and milk.

# DIET SWAPS

Replacing animal products for plant-based produce will open up a world of wonderful possibilities.

## MILK AND DAIRY PRODUCTS

Not all milks are from animals such as soy, rice, and almond. They are all low in fat and make a wonderful alternative, providing you with the same creamy texture that you would find in dairy milk. There is a vast array of vegan alternatives to dairy-based products for you to explore. Some dairy replacement products are so delicious that they have been adopted by meat-eaters too.

## MEAT OR SAUSAGES REPLACEMENT

Fermented soybeans known as tempeh is full of protein and is easily available. Tofu is also very common and can be pressed to be rid of excess moisture then marinated to retain flavor. You will find that due to the growth of veganism your supermarkets will have numerous meat replacements, usually in the freezer aisle, that taste excellent and mimic the texture of meat very closely.

## EGGS

Eggs are one of the most difficult ingredients to substitute. The key is to think about the function they performed in the recipes. If you are looking for a binding agent - cornstarch, arrowroot, tahini, bread crumbs and mashed potatoes are good

replacements. If you need a raising agent baking powder usually works well. There are many alternative products on the market including a powder which makes delicious scrambled 'eggs', as well as various egg replacers which are suitable for baking.

So go ahead and veganise your dishes - you won't even notice the difference!

# HOW TO STAY HEALTHY ON A VEGAN DIET?

Our meal patterns are commonly based on three meals a day. Health experts have recognised that five to seven smaller meals throughout the day are better as it helps to keep blood sugar levels even.

You can even lose weight by eating more often as smaller portions are easier to digest and keep your metabolism working for longer.

## BREAKFAST

It's sensible to start the day with a solid and varied breakfast, no matter which diet you are on. Cereal and fresh fruits are the easiest. In India, people often start the day with a kind of bread and vegetables (see our sides recipes and try out the Paratha or Besan Cheela).

The perfect breakfast recipe would be the Besan Cheela (Eggless omelet filled with vegetables). This will certainly fill you up and avoid any mid-morning snacking.

If you prefer a sweet breakfast to a savoury one go for a fruit packed smoothie, vegetable juice or a lassi. 'Love Vegan: The Essential Indian Cookbook for Vegans' has a wonderful recipe for a lassi, and you can alternate the fruit used within it according to what is in season or what you have to hand.

## MID-MORNING

Don't wait for hunger to strike, as you are more likely to make the wrong food choices. Instead opt pt for seeds, nuts, and cut up vegetables and dips (refer to our chutney and side sections for inspiration)

## LUNCH

For lunch, pick one of our mains or sides such as curries, dhals, tofu dishes, salads and soups, it's all there for your picking. It's always a great idea to make extra the night before so that you have leftovers ready for your lunch.

Mid afternoon have another snack of fruits and nuts, or try our Warm Turmeric & Cinnamon Milk or a Mango Lassi to curb any cravings.

## DINNER

Follow this up with a main dish and side for dinner. Don't hold back, our recipes are quick and easy to prepare. A prominent ingredient in vegan Indian food are pulses so you will find many of the recipes feature beans, lentils or chickpeas. These are very filling and a fantastic source of fibre. Indian dishes are commonly served with white rice, however, for a more nutritious side opt for brown or black rice.

# HEALTH AND NUTRITIONAL BENEFITS

'The food you eat can be either the safest and most powerful form of medicine or the slowest form of poison' - Ann Wigmore

Not only does the vegan diet provide numerous health benefits including a reduced risk of contracting heart disease, obesity, hypertension and diabetes, it also provides social, moral and environmental benefits.

When adopting a vegan lifestyle it is important to know a few basic facts about nutrition, and to be careful when planning meals by making sure that your diet contains not only plenty of vegetables and fresh fruits, but also whole grains, beans, legumes, nuts and seeds. A vegan diet should be pack with B1, C, and E, folic acid, magnesium and iron.

Let take a look at the various vegan sources for these different vitamins and minerals so that you can perfectly balance your vegan diet:

## VITAMIN B

A vegan diet is packed with vitamin B which is found in fresh fruits and vegetables. There are several kinds of sources for vitamin B but the most reliable sources include:

- Pulses
- Beans
- Whole grains
- Potatoes
- Banana
- Nutritional yeast
- Chili peppers

## VITAMIN B12

Sourcing vitamin B12 poses difficulties for vegans as it is commonly found in animal products, so in order to eliminate any problems, your diet might have to be complemented with either fortified food or supplements.

## VITAMIN C

Essential for strong bones and teeth, vitamin C is found in food items such as:

- Tomato and tomato sauces
- Dark leafy greens
- Fresh juices
- Cereals
- Berries

## VITAMIN E

Like all other vitamins, Vitamin E plays many roles, among others it has an important neurological function and is responsible for repairing tissues and wounds.

The best sources of Vitamin E for vegans are:

- Oils (Olive, Coconut, Nut oils)
- Avocados
- Kiwis
- Tomatoes
- Pumpkins
- Mangoes
- Papayas

## IRON

Many vegetables contain iron. It is very important to include iron in your diet as it is essential for blood production. Iron is synonymous with Popeye's fondness for spinach but did you know that the following are packed with Iron too:

- Potatoes
- Lentils
- Almond
- Flax and pumpkin seeds
- Chickpeas

# DISCOVER THE FLAVORS OF INDIA

India is a vast country with wide regional variations. The cuisines of India are as multifaceted and wide ranging as its multi-ethnic cultures. The delicious and exotic dishes of India have one common denominator which is their subtle uses of spices and herbs.

It is often said that cooking Indian food is complicated and needs a lot of special ingredients, but actually, Indian recipes are very simple to make. 'Love Vegan: The Essential Indian Cookbook for Vegans' explores this diverse cuisine and makes it easy to recreate in your very own kitchen.

In India, every region has their own specialities. There are few similarities between the traditional dishes of the four cardinal points of this vast land, but again all the regions are united by their love of spices.

Traditionally, Indians eat at home or more accurately at one another's home, as food plays an important role in the social and religious calendar. Restaurants and simple eateries are always buzzing too. Night markets are a joy and a means to discover all sorts of delicious dishes.

Let's take a look at some of the flavors and staple dishes from around the country and see how easy it is to adapt them to the vegan diet, while still retaining the taste, texture and lively Indian flavor.

## SOUTH-INDIAN CUISINE

In the 5 states which constitute South India, the cuisine includes lots of lentils, spices and tends to be chili-hot. The addition of coconut is typical of South-Indian cuisine. Exotic fruits grow abundantly here, including wonderful, fleshy mangoes and for this reason chutneys are very popular in South India.

## NORTH-INDIAN CUISINE

Most restaurants we know in the West serve North-Indian dishes. The kind which is prepared in the Punjab such as creamy curries and "butter dish". You will find that one of our first recipe in the mains is a Creamy Vegan Korma which can seriously rival any meat based version of the curry.

## CUISINE FROM THE EASTERN REGIONS

Due to its climate, the east of India is a rice growing area. Not surprisingly, rice and vegetables form a major part of the cuisine. This is where the use of spices comes to its own. Our 'Bengali' Chana Masala is a perfect example of a typical East-Indian dish.

## CENTRAL AND WESTERN CUISINES

Two of the many popular dishes are Burfi and Biryani. Here is where snacks come to their own, for example Bhajis and Tikki are regional dishes. When it comes to mains, the dishes are a mixture of Northern and Southern influences.

# AROMATIC & FRAGRANT INDIAN SPICES

The history of spices is woven into the trade history. Fortunes were made thanks to cloves, pepper and nutmeg. Tall tales of impossible to reach areas, infested with snakes were invented and rich spice locations were a closely guarded secret for centuries.

The medicinal properties and health benefits of spices have been recognised for a long time. The traditional Ayurvedic medicine of India has roots in herbs and spices. Scientific studies suggest that some ingredients specific to India can help prevent deadly illnesses.

Have a look at some useful spices for your larder:

## CUMIN

Strongly aromatic, the taste will change whether cumin is fried or dried roasted. The seeds are used at the end of a meal as a digestive and will often be passed around in a tray.

## CORIANDER POWDER

All the parts of the coriander plant are used in Indian cooking. The seeds are used to thicken dishes and the fresh leaves to ornate and decorate.

## Turmeric

Very similar to ginger, this root is the spice which gives the Indian dishes their beautiful yellow hue. It is arguably one of the most powerful spices in terms of its healing properties.

## CHILI POWDER

Varies in levels of heat. It's worth experimenting with various brands to find a chili powder you like, as not only do they vary in heat but also in taste. Chilies are also a rich source of vitamin C.

## CURRY POWDER

Oddly enough curry powder is is a bit of a fraud as it's actually a western invention! There is no such as thing as Curry Powder in the natural world. Curry Powder is a blend which contains mostly and as a base, coriander, turmeric, cumin, fenugreek, and chili peppers then depending on the recipe, additional ingredients such as ginger and garlic are also included.

With time, you will learn which of the spices you like and and perhaps you will even make your own jar of curry powder!

## CINNAMON STICKS

Cinnamon sticks are carved from the bark of the cinnamon tree, and commonly used in sweet dishes, however, the flavor is also delicious in savoury dishes

## MUSTARD SEEDS

Often recipes use the whole seeds which are fried quickly in oil in order to bring out their flavor but be aware, seeds tend to pop all over the place in the process.

## CARDAMON

Sweet and spicy with a strong flavor, cardamom is used both in sweet and savoury dishes. If you want to impress your diners use the black variety which is used seldom in Europe or the States but commonly added to dishes in India.

# INDIAN STAPLE PANTRY ITEMS

When cooking vegan versions of Indian cuisine, pulses and legumes are a good substitute for meat. They can be made into delicious side dishes, used as the star ingredient in curries or even served alone. Tinned beans are a great staple to have in your pantry cupboard. Make sure you have a wide selection and try them all to find your favourites.

To make your life easier and to ensure your kitchen is equipt with staple items most commonly used in Indian cooking, it is advisable that you have a well-stocked pantry to avoid a last minute trip to the supermarket after a long day at work.

The list below is a variety of simple and straightforward ingredients that you should keep in your cupboards, so that you are ready to whip up a delicious authentic Indian dish at any time.

Basmati rice
Plain and gram flour
Chickpeas
Lentils
Beans
Tinned coconut milk
Tinned chopped tomatoes
Lemon / Lime
Ginger
Garlic
Fresh cilantro
Vegetable oil
Raw nuts
Onions
Tofu
Potatoes
Fresh and frozen vegetables

# LOVE VEGAN

## QUICK AND EASY TO PREPARE

Nobody wants to spend hours in the kitchen to make dinner following a long, hard day. This is a good reason to include Indian food as a staple cuisine in your household. A lot of the dishes are fast and easy to prepare despite a relatively long ingredient list, however, most need to simmer for a while but that doesn't require your presence.

There are also lots of advantages to vegan Indian cuisine. Traditionally vegetable based, it's an excellent diet for slimmers and will provide you with limitless vitality whilst leaving you full and satisfied.

The vast majority of recipes provided in this cookbook can be made in half an hour or less. Who wouldn't like to tuck in an Aloo Baingan Sabzi aka Eggplant Curry or a Palak Tofu with a side dish of Authentic Indian Spiced Potato and Pea Parathas, washed down with a Mango Lassi. This book contains snappy, simple and flavorsome recipes- the Love Vegan Indian way.

## RECIPES FOR ALL OCCASIONS

Indian cooking is exceptionally well fitted for all sorts of events. In India, people love to share their meals with friends and family and eating is a big part of religious celebrations too. When in their own kitchen, before starting a recipe, Indian cooks lay out all the ingredients on the worktop and that includes little bowls with each spice required for the dish.

There is enough variety in one Indian meal to satisfy the pickiest of eaters. Usually meals consist of a main dish, a dhal, one or two vegetable dishes and a raita or chutney. The dessert usually consists of a fruit, and sweets and cakes are reserved for special occasions. Every meal is served with rice as well as flatbread. This formula can be adapted to serve many occasions.

With a bit of practice, you'll make these dishes your own and your inventiveness will shine through! For instance, you could have a go at making Crispy Eggplant Bhaji's for an inviting change rather than the Crispy Zucchini Bhajis.

## WHOLESOME, NATURAL INGREDIENTS

Indian recipes have relied on fresh and natural ingredients for centuries. You will not need to run around searching for the ingredients within our recipes as they are straightforward and everything you need can be found in farmers' market or your local supermarket.

Indians use spices to enhance the flavors of raw vegetables but also to protect against food-borne infection. If at first you need to invest in jars of spices, don't worry, you will be able to use the spices again and again, and will be surprised at how long they last.

The aim of this book and the Love Vegan series is to make eating and cooking food, which is good for your body, a pleasure and to cut down on the fuss of preparation.

## TRIED AND TESTED RECIPES

All the recipes in this book have been carefully tried and tested. Often they are recipes which have been passed down from generations of cooks. We have taken all the Indian classics and have slightly adapted them to remove animal products. Since a lot of Indians are vegetarian to start with, our dishes are authentic and retain the tastes and flavors of the subcontinent.

The best thing about cooking vegan foods is that most variations of classic Indian foods will only take a fraction of the time that cooking the meat or fish versions would have taken.

## SUMMARY

Indian cuisine is a fusion of various cultures from all over the country and it boasts a very rich history.

So if you thought Indian food was all about meat and dairy think again! You can see from this cookbook that an exotic and inspirational Indian vegan food journey awaits you in the recipes that follow.

# MAINS

# MUSHROOM MATAR MASALA

This restaurant style recipe originates in Punjabi, Northern India and combines tender mushrooms and fresh peas with a wonderfully creamy and flavorsome thick sauce.

**Preparation Time**
10 minutes (+30 minutes to soak the cashews)

**Total Time**
35 minutes

**Makes**
4 servings

## INGREDIENTS

1 small onion, roughly chopped
6 cloves garlic
1 ½ inch ginger
2 green chilis (seeds removed depending on heat preference)
1 tsp oil
4 large tomatoes
½ cup raw cashews (soaked for 30 minutes in boiling water)
1 tsp garam masala
1 tsp coriander powder

1 tsp paprika
1 ½ tsp dried fenugreek leaves
½ tsp turmeric
1 tsp salt
½ tsp sugar
12oz / 340g sliced mushrooms (white, chestnut or portobello)
1 ¼ cup peas, fresh or frozen
1 cup spinach, washed
½ cup loosely packed cilantro, rough chopped

## DIRECTIONS

Place onion, garlic, ginger, chilies and 2 tablespoons of water in a blender and pulse until a smooth paste forms, scraping down the edges as you go along.

Transfer the puree into a medium pan and cook over medium heat, stirring frequently, for 6-7 minutes. Add a dash of water if it starts to dry out or stick to the bottom.

Place tomatoes and cashew nuts in the blender (no need to wash) and pulse for 1-2 minutes until smooth.

Stir the garam masala, paprika, cilantro, fenugreek, turmeric powder, salt, and sugar into the onion puree and cook for a minute then pour in the blended tomato-cashew mixture, frying for 7-8 minutes and stirring occasionally.

Add the mushrooms and peas, cover and cook for 10 minutes over a low heat until the mushrooms are tender. Stir in the cilantro and spinach and serve once it has wilted.

# CREAMY CASHEW & COCONUT KORMA

This creamy, nutty and exotic curry is made with vegetables and sweet potatoes, and simmered in a rich Indian spiced coconut sauce. It's simple to make and the sweet mildly spiced flavor is a favorite with adults and children alike.

**Preparation Time**
25 minutes

**Total Time**
55 minutes

**Makes**
4 servings

## INGREDIENTS

1 ½ tbsp vegetable oil
1 small onion, finely chopped
1 tsp fresh ginger, grated
4 garlic cloves, minced
1 ½ tbsp curry powder
1 tsp ground cumin
1 tsp turmeric
1 tsp ground coriander
1 medium sweet potatoes, peeled and cubed
4 carrots, chopped
1 fresh green chili, seeded and chopped

2 tbsp ground unsalted almonds or cashew nuts
½ cup passata or tomato sauce
2 cups frozen diced vegetables
1 cup coconut milk
½ cup vegetable stock
½ tsp coarse salt
½ tsp freshly ground pepper
½ cup fresh cilantro, roughly chopped

## DIRECTIONS

Heat the oil in the large saucepan over medium heat. Saute the onions for 2-3 minutes until soft and tender then add the garlic, ginger and chilis and cook for a minute. Add the curry powder, cumin, turmeric and coriander and stir constantly for another minute.

Add potatoes, carrots, ground nuts, passata, stock and coconut milk and bring the mixture to a boil. Reduce to a simmer and allow the liquid to thicken and reduce for 10 minutes. Season with salt and pepper then add frozen vegetables and cook for a further 10-15 minutes until the potatoes are cooked.

Garnish with cilantro and serve immediately while hot.

# ALOO BAINGAN SABZI (EGGPLANT CURRY)

This simple and healthy eggplant curry is perfect served over basmati rice or with naan bread. The silky texture of the eggplant makes this curry a really satisfying and delicious meal.

**Preparation Time**
10 minutes

**Total Time**
25 minutes

**Makes**
2 servings as a main or 4 as a side

## INGREDIENTS

1 large eggplant, cut into ¾ inch cubes
1 large potato, peeled and cut into ¾ inch cubes
1 large onion, finely chopped
2 medium tomatoes, finely chopped
1 ½ tbsp oil
1 tsp cumin seeds
1 tsp mustard seeds

1-inch fresh ginger, peeled and grated
2 garlic cloves, minced
¼ tsp turmeric
½ tsp red chili powder
1 tsp coriander powder
½ tsp coarse salt
2-3 tbsp fresh cilantro leaves to garnish

## DIRECTIONS

Heat oil in a large saucepan over medium heat and add cumin and mustard seeds. Once the seeds start to crackle add onions and saute for 3-4 minutes until they become soft. Add ginger, garlic, turmeric, chili powder and coriander powder and fry for a minute.

Add tomatoes and stir frequently for 2 minutes until they have softened. Carefully add potatoes and eggplant to the pot and stir to coat. Reduce heat to low, cover with a lid and cook for 10 minutes. Check on the vegetables after 5 minutes to see they are not drying out. If the appear to be dry add a splash of water.

Once the potatoes are tender when pierced with a fork remove from heat, transfer to a serving bowl and garnish with cilantro.

# INDIAN DOSA WITH SPICED POTATO STUFFING

Dosa is a staple part of the South Indian diet and is made up of a thin, savory 'crepe' made of rice and urad dhal flour that is filled with a potato based stuffing.

**Preparation Time**
10 minutes (+ overnight for the batter to ferment)

**Total Time**
25 minutes

**Makes**
2 servings

## INGREDIENTS

FOR THE DOSA

1 ½ cups rice flour
¾ cup urad dhal flour (black gram flour)
2 ½ cups water
½ tsp salt

FOR THE STUFFING

2 medium potatoes, quartered
1 tbsp vegetable oil

1 tsp cumin seeds
1 tsp mustard seeds
1 white onion, finely chopped
1-inch fresh ginger, grated
1 tsp ground coriander
1 tsp ground turmeric
½ tsp salt
½ tsp pepper
1 tbsp freshly squeezed lemon juice
2 heaped tbsp fresh cilantro, roughly chopped

## DIRECTIONS

TO MAKE THE DOSA:

In a large mixing bowl mix the rice flour and urad dhal then pour in water, mixing well until you have a smooth, lump-free batter. Cover and allow the batter to ferment for a minimum of

8 hours, or preferably overnight.

Once the batter has fermented mix in the salt.

Heat a non stick pan with a little oil and once hot pour in a ladle of batter, and gently spread the dosa in circular rounds. Allow the dosa to brown on one side then flip it over and cook the other side.

Continue with the remaining batter. The batter will keep for 3-4 days in the fridge if you do not wish to use it all.

TO MAKE THE POTATO STUFFING:

Place potatoes in a large pan and cover with enough cold water to fully submerge them. Bring to a boil then simmer for 6-7 minutes until tender when pierced with a fork. Remove from the heat and drain the potatoes.

Heat a tablespoon of oil over medium heat and fry the cumin and mustard seeds until they start to become fragrant and the mustard seeds begin to pop. Add the chopped onion and sauté for 10 minutes until soft, then add the ginger, coriander, turmeric, salt, and pepper, stirring constantly for 1 minute.

Add the potatoes to the mixture with 2 tablespoons of water and gently crush them using a fork until most of the potatoes have broken down. Give everything a good mix, adding another tablespoon of water if it feels a little dry.

Squeeze in the lemon juice and stir in the fresh cilantro.

Serve with the dosa wraps.

# PUNJABI MATAR 'PANEER' (TOFU AND PEA CURRY)

A simple and easy recipe that features tender tofu and sweet crisp peas that have been simmering in a mildly spiced tomato based gravy. Perfect served with naan, roti or chapatis.

| **Preparation Time** | **Total Time** | **Makes** |
|:---:|:---:|:---:|
| 10 minutes | 30 minutes | 4 servings |

## INGREDIENTS

10.5oz / 300g firm tofu
2 tbsp vegetable, canola or sunflower oil, divided
1 tsp cumin seeds
1 tsp coriander seeds
1 large white onion, finely chopped
2 cloves garlic, crushed
1-inch piece ginger, grated
2 tbsp curry powder
½ tsp turmeric powder

1 tsp salt
4 large ripe tomatoes, roughly chopped
2 cups water or vegetable stock
2 cups peas, frozen
1 tbsp lemon juice
¼ cup fresh cilantro leaves, roughly chopped

## DIRECTIONS

To start, remove tofu from packaging and press between two towels to remove excess water. You can use something weighted, such as a large saucepan or a heavy chopping board and place this on top of the tofu to squeeze out as much moisture as possible for a minimum of 10 minutes. This process will allow the tofu to absorb much more flavor. After 10 minutes chop tofu into small cubes.

Heat a skillet with 1 tablespoon vegetable oil and fry over

medium-high heat for 4-5 minutes until golden on either side. Remove and set aside on a paper towel lined plate.

Heat the same skillet you used to fry the tofu with 1 tablespoon of oil and add the cumin and coriander seeds. Fry for 1-2 minutes until they become fragrant then add the chopped onion. Saute the onion for 5-6 minutes until soft then add the garlic, ginger, curry powder, turmeric, and salt and stir for a minute.

Add the chopped tomatoes, frying for 2-3 minutes until the tomatoes start to soften then pour in the water. Cover and cook for 15 minutes then add the peas and tofu cubes, cooking for 2-3 minutes until the peas have defrosted and the tofu has heated.

Remove from the heat and add lemon juice and chopped cilantro.

Serve with rice or chapattis.

# SWEET POTATO & CHICKPEA TIKKA MASALA

A beautiful vegan version of an Indian favourite. The curry features chickpeas, vegetables and sweet potatoes, all simmering in a rich, creamy and aromatic sauce. It's almost foolproof to make and takes only 10 minutes to prepare.

| **Preparation Time** | **Total Time** | **Makes** |
|---|---|---|
| 10 minutes | 35 minutes | 4 servings |

## INGREDIENTS

5 whole cardamom pods
½ tsp cardamom seeds
4 medium white onions, chopped
3 garlic cloves, crushed
1 tsp ginger, grated
4-5 curry leaves
1 green chili, deseeded and chopped
½ tsp ground cinnamon
1 tsp garam masala
1 tsp turmeric
1 tsp Tandoori Masala powder
1 tsp paprika
1 tsp curry powder
1 large sweet potato, peeled and chopped into 1-inch chunks

2 medium carrots
1 tin of chickpeas, drained and rinsed
½ red pepper, chopped
½ yellow pepper, chopped
2 tbsp coconut cream
1 cup vegetable stock
1 tin chopped tomatoes
1 tbsp tomato puree
2 tbsp vegetable oil
1 tsp sugar
½ tsp coarse salt
½ tsp freshly ground black pepper
2 tbsp fresh cilantro, roughly chopped

# DIRECTIONS

In a large saucepan heat oil over medium heat and add 3 cardamom pods and cumin seeds. Once the cardamom seeds start to darken add onions and allow them to caramelise for around 15 minutes. Once caramelised add cinnamon, garlic, ginger and chili and fry for 1 minute.

Push the onion mixture to the very edge of the frying pan and add the garam masala, turmeric, tandoori masala, paprika and curry powder and fry in the center of the pan for 1-2 minutes.

Add the tomato puree then mix the spices and onions together, stirring frequently for 1 minute.

Pour in tinned tomatoes, stock, coconut cream, potatoes, carrots, seasoning and sugar, and bring to a boil. Reduce to a simmer and cook for 10 minutes.

Add the peppers and chickpeas and simmer for a further 15 minutes until the carrots and sweet potatoes are tender when pierced with a fork and the sauce has thickened and reduced.

Transfer to a serving bowl and garnish with cilantro.

Serve immediately over freshly cooked rice.

# RICH & CREAMY 'BUTTER CHICKEN'

Tofu makes a wonderful substitute for chicken in this vegan version of a classic Indian dish. Blending cashew nuts with non-dairy milk gives the curry a rich creamy texture that can rival any dairy based version.

**Preparation Time**
10 minutes (+ 10 minutes to press tofu)

**Total Time**
35 minutes

**Makes**
4 servings

## INGREDIENTS

¾ cup raw unsalted cashews
¾ cup unsweetened almond or soy milk
2 tbsp vegetable oil
1 tbsp fresh ginger, grated
3 clove garlic, minced
1 medium onion, finely chopped
1 fresh green chili
½-1 tsp chili powder
1 tsp turmeric
1 tsp ground coriander
1 tsp cumin

½ tsp cinnamon
1 tbsp brown sugar or maple syrup
1 can chopped tomatoes
½ cup vegetable stock
1 package extra firm tofu
½ tsp coarse salt
½ tsp freshly ground black pepper
1 tbsp freshly squeezed lemon juice
Handful of fresh cilantro, chopped

## DIRECTIONS

To start, remove tofu from packaging and press between two towels to remove excess water. You can use something weighted, such as a large saucepan or chopping board and place this on top of the tofu to squeeze out as much moisture as possible for a minimum of 10 minutes. This process will allow the tofu to absorb much more flavor. After 10 minutes chop tofu into small cubes. Set aside.

Place the cashew nuts and non-dairy milk in a blender or food processor and blend until completely smooth and lump-free. Set aside.

Heat a large pan with oil over medium heat. Saute onions for 2-3 minutes until softened then add ginger, garlic and chilis, frying for 30 seconds. Add the chili powder, turmeric, ground coriander, cumin, cinnamon and stir constantly for another 30 seconds.

Pour in the chopped tomato, brown sugar, stock, cashew mix and pressed tofu, mixing well to combine.

Simmer for around 20 minutes until the liquid has thickened and reduced.

Remove from heat, transfer to a serving bowl and garnish with chopped cilantro.

Serve with fresh basmati rice or naan bread.

# SRI LANKAN COCONUT & CAULIFLOWER CURRY

Sri Lankan curries are not for the timid eater! They usually pack a fiery punch and are bursting with flavor. This curry is cooled down slightly with creamy coconut milk, making it more suitable for everyday dinners.

**Preparation Time**
10 minutes

**Total Time**
30 minutes

**Makes**
4 servings

## INGREDIENTS

4 tbsp vegetable, sunflower or canola oil
½ tsp fennel seeds
1 tsp cumin seeds
1 tsp coriander seeds
1 tsp black mustard seeds
1 medium white onion, sliced
4 garlic cloves, finely chopped
2 green chilies, finely chopped
2-inch piece of fresh ginger, grated
1 tbsp curry powder
10 curry leaves
1 tsp turmeric

1 cinnamon stick
2 cups / 475ml vegetable stock
2 tbsp soy sauce
1 tsp salt
7oz / 200g butternut squash, cubed
1 small cauliflower, cut into florets
1 large carrot, chopped
2 x 14oz / 400g can coconut milk
1 lime, juiced
½ cup fresh cilantro, roughly chopped

## DIRECTIONS

Heat a large skillet with oil and add fennel, cumin, coriander and mustard seeds, stirring for 1 minute until fragrant and the mustard seeds start to pop. Add the chopped onion and sauté for 3-4 minutes until soft.

Add garlic, ginger, and chilies and fry for 30 seconds, stirring frequently to prevent burning, then add the curry powder, curry leaves, turmeric, and cinnamon, stirring again for another minute.

Pour in the stock, soy sauce, and salt along with all of the vegetables and bring to a boil. Reduce to a simmer and cook, uncovered, for 10 minutes until the vegetables start to soften.

Pour in both cans of coconut milk and give everything a good stir. Cook uncovered for another 10 minutes until the sauce begins to thicken and reduce.

Remove from the heat, and add lime juice and cilantro before serving.

Serve over rice.

# GOAN VINDALOO TOFU

Vindaloo curry originates in Goa and is known for its distinctly spicy sauce. You can substitute the tofu for any filling you wish such as potatoes or chickpeas in this versatile dish.

**Preparation Time**
25 minutes (+ 10 minutes to press the tofu)

**Total Time**
45 minutes

**Makes**
4 servings

## INGREDIENTS

3 tbsp vegetable oil
2-inch piece fresh ginger, peeled and minced
2 large garlic cloves, peeled and minced
2 medium onions, chopped
½ head cauliflower, stem removed and cut into florets
½ cup fresh green beans, sliced
3 medium carrots, peeled and chopped

3 tbsp vindaloo curry powder
6 tbsp tomato puree
1 (14oz / 420g) can coconut milk
1 cup vegetable stock
1 (14oz / 420g) can chickpeas, drained and rinsed
1 lb / 450g extra-firm tofu, cut into 1-inch cubes
½ tsp coarse salt
¼ tsp freshly ground pepper

## DIRECTIONS

To start, remove tofu from packaging and press between two towels to remove excess water. You can use something weighted, such as a large saucepan or chopping board and place this on top of the tofu to squeeze out as much moisture as possible for a minimum of 10 minutes. This process will allow the tofu to absorb much more flavor. After 10 minutes chop tofu into small cubes. Set aside.

Heat oil in a large frying pan over medium-high heat. Saute the onions for 2-3 minutes then add the garlic and ginger, stirring constantly for 30 seconds.

Add the cauliflower and carrots and cook for around 5-6 minutes until the vegetables have softened.

Stir in the vindaloo powder and the tomato puree and fry for 30 seconds, stirring constantly.

Pour in the coconut milk, stock, chickpeas, tofu and green beans. Bring mixture to a simmer then reduce to low and cook for 15-20 minutes until the liquid has reduced and thickened.

Season with salt and pepper and serve with freshly cooked basmati rice.

# CREAMY CURRIED SPINACH & CHICKPEAS

A healthy and filling vegan meal that's brimming with vitamins and nutrients from the spinach and chickpeas. The creamy sauce is made from cashew nuts and non-dairy milk and added to the fragrant and exotically spiced vegetables.

**Preparation Time**
10 minutes

**Total Time**
25 minutes

**Makes**
4-6 servings

## INGREDIENTS

2 tbsp vegetable or olive oil
1 large onion, chopped
4 cloves garlic, finely chopped
1 tbsp fresh ginger, grated
1 small fresh green chili, finely chopped
1 tsp cumin seeds
2 tsp garam masala
1 tsp coriander powder
1 tsp turmeric
½ tsp dried chili flakes
8 cups / 7oz / 200g fresh spinach , washed and chopped

½ cup vegetable broth
1 cup unsweetened soy or almond milk
¼ cup raw unsalted cashews
2 ½ tbsp tomato paste
½ tsp sugar
2 cans chickpeas, drained and rinsed
½ tsp coarse salt
¼ tsp freshly ground black pepper

## DIRECTIONS

Heat a large pot with vegetable oil over medium heat. Once hot saute onions for 2-3 minutes. Add the ginger, garlic and fresh chili and fry for 1 minute. Add the cumin seeds, garam masala, coriander powder, turmeric and dried chili flakes and stir constantly for 30 seconds.

Reduce the heat to low, stir in the spinach and stock, cover the pot and cook for 5-6 minutes until the spinach has wilted.

While the spinach is cooking place the cashew nuts, non-dairy milk, sugar, tomato paste and nutritional yeast (if using) in a food processor and blend until smooth.

Once the spinach has cooked for 5-6 minutes, uncover the pot and pour in the cashew-milk mixture along with the chickpeas, salt and pepper and mix well to combine.

Simmer uncovered for 7-10 minutes.

Serve with hot basmati rice or naan bread.

# BAINGAN BHARTA
## (SOFT ROASTED & SPICED EGGPLANTS)

This Indian dish can be compared to Baba Ganoush as its similarities lie in the soft roasted and mashed eggplants combined with aromatic Indian spices, chili and tomato.

**Preparation Time**
10 minutes

**Total Time**
35 minutes

**Makes**
4-6 servings

## INGREDIENTS

17.5oz / 500g eggplant
1 tbsp olive oil
1 medium white onion, chopped
1 large garlic clove, finely chopped
1-inch piece of ginger, grated
½ tsp garam masala
½ tsp turmeric

1 tsp ground coriander powder
1 small green chili, finely chopped (seeds removed depending on heat preference)
1 large ripe tomato, chopped
¾ tsp salt

## DIRECTIONS

Preheat the oven to 430°c.

Prick the eggplant a few times then roast until the skin is charred and the inner flesh is soft. A good way of testing whether the flesh is soft is to pierce the eggplant with the end of a spoon. Set aside until cool enough to touch then peel and discard the skin and mash the flesh in a bowl.

While the eggplant is cooling down heat oil over a medium flame and sauté the onions for 5 minutes. Add garlic, ginger, garam masala, turmeric, coriander, chili and the chopped tomato and give everything a good stir. Fry for 5 minutes, adding a splash of water if the mixture appears to be drying out.

Stir in the mashed eggplant and salt, and fry until heated throughout.

Serve with naan, chapatis or rice.

# PEA, CAULIFLOWER & POTATO DHAL

A unique take on a traditional Indian dish with the addition of peas and cauliflower. This meal is cheap, delicious and healthy, and sure to become a staple on your dinner table.

**Preparation Time**
10 minutes

**Total Time**
50 minutes

**Makes**
4 servings

## INGREDIENTS

½ onion, finely chopped
1 large potato, washed, peeled and cubed
1 small head of cauliflower, stem removed and cut into florets
2 cups frozen or fresh peas
1 ½ cups split red lentil, washed
1 small onion, finely chopped
2-3 garlic cloves, minced
1-inch fresh ginger, grated
1 fresh green chili, thinly sliced
4 cups vegetable stock
2 tbsp vegetable oil
2 bay leaf

5 cardamon pods, slightly crushed
1 small cinnamon stick
1 ½ tsp turmeric
1 tsp garam masala
1 tsp chili powder
1 ½ tsp cumin powder
1 tsp coriander powder
½ tsp fennel powder (optional)
1 tsp coarse salt
½ tsp freshly ground black pepper
2 tbsp fresh cilantro, chopped
½ lemon, freshly squeezed

## DIRECTIONS

Pour stock into a large saucepan and bring to a boil. Once the liquid has come to a rolling boil add the lentils, bay leaves, cardamom and cinnamon stick. Reduce heat to a simmer and cook for around 20-25 minutes or until the liquid has reduced and the lentils are soft and tender.

While the lentils are cooking heat a large skillet with vegetable oil and fry the onions for 2-3 minutes until soft then add the garlic, ginger and fresh chilies, frying for 30 seconds. Add the turmeric, garam masala, chili powder, cumin, coriander and fennel powder and cook for 1 minute until fragrant.

Add the potatoes, peas and cauliflower and mix to combine. Fry on medium-low for 15-20 minutes until the potatoes are tender.

Once the lentils have cooked discard the liquid, but reserve 1/3 cup. Add the lentils and 1/3 cup of lentil stock to the potato mixture along with salt, pepper, cilantro and the freshly squeezed lemon juice.

Serve with fresh basmati rice or naan bread.

# 'BENGALI' CHANA MASALA

A quick and easy spiced chickpea and tomato dish, perfect served over freshly made basmati rice.

| **Preparation Time** | **Total Time** | **Makes** |
|---|---|---|
| 15 minutes | 35 minutes | 4 servings |

## INGREDIENTS

1 tbsp olive or vegetable oil
2 tsp cumin seeds
1 tsp mustard seeds
1 medium onion, chopped
3 cloves garlic, finely chopped
1 tbsp fresh ginger, grated
1 large green chili, chopped (seeds removed to reduce the heat)
1 tbsp garam masala
1 heaped tsp ground coriander
1 tsp ground turmeric
¼ tsp chili powder

2 (2 x 14oz / 420g) can chopped tomatoes
¼ tsp sugar
2 (2 x 14oz / 420g) can chickpeas
½ tsp coarse salt
½ tsp freshly ground black pepper
1 cup uncooked basmati rice
2 cups water + 1 tsp salt
1 tbsp freshly squeezed lemon juice
2 tbsp fresh cilantro, roughly chopped

## DIRECTIONS

In a large skillet heat the oil over medium heat. Once hot add the cumin and mustard seeds, stirring frequently for 30 seconds. Once the mustard seeds start to pop add the onions and saute for 2-3 minutes until soft. Add the garlic, ginger and chili and cook for a minute.

Stir in the garam masala, turmeric, chili powder and coriander powder and fry for 1-2 minutes, then pour in both cans of chopped tomatoes and ¼ tsp sugar.

Bring mixture to a boil then reduce to a simmer. Stir in the two cans of chickpeas and cook for 15-20 minutes for the sauce to reduce and thicken.

While the mixture is cooking add 2 cups of salted water to a medium saucepan and bring to a boil. Add rice, reduce to a simmer and cover. Cook rice for 17-20 minutes.

Remove chana masala from the heat and stir in 1 tbsp lemon juice. Add to a large serving bowl and garnish with cilantro.

Serve hot over rice.

# DAL MAKHANI
# (BLACK LENTILS WITH RICH TOMATO SAUCE)

Dal Makhani originates from Punjab but has become popular throughout the Western world. It consists of black lentils and kidney beans in an authentic and aromatic tomato sauce. Be sure to keep any leftovers as the curry tastes even better the following day.

**Preparation Time**
15 minutes (+ overnight for lentils and beans to soak)

**Total Time**
45 minutes

**Makes**
6 servings

## INGREDIENTS

1 cup dried black lentils
1 cup dried pinto or kidney beans
3 tbsp olive or vegetable oil
2 medium onions, chopped
6 large cloves garlic, minced
1-inch piece fresh ginger, grated
2 bay leaves
1 cinnamon stick
3 cardamom pods
2 dried red chili peppers or 1 tsp dried chili flakes

1½ tbsp garam masala
1 tsp ground coriander
1 tsp cumin seeds
¾ tsp chili powder
1 tsp paprika
¼ tsp ground black pepper
1 tsp coarse salt
1 (14oz / 420g) can chopped tomatoes
6 tbsp tomato puree
2 cups vegetable stock

## DIRECTIONS

Add the lentils and beans to a large bowl, pour in enough water to just cover them and leave to soak overnight. Drain and discard the water the following day and give the lentils and beans a quick rinse.

Transfer the soaked lentils and beans to a medium saucepan and fill with just enough water to cover. Add ½ tsp salt and bring to a boil. Reduce to a simmer and cook covered for 45 minutes, checking regularly to see whether you need to add a splash more water. Once cooked, remove from heat, drain and discard water and set aside.

Around 20 minutes before the beans and lentils have finished cooking heat oil in a large saucepan over medium heat. Add onions and stir well to coat with oil. Allow onions to cook for 12-15 minutes to caramelise, stirring regularly.

Add garlic, ginger, dried chili, bay leaves, cardamom, cinnamon, garam masala, coriander, cumin, paprika and chili powder. Cook for 1 ½ minutes stirring constantly.

Pour in chopped tomatoes, tomato puree, vegetable stock, beans/lentils and seasoning and bring to a boil. Reduce to a low simmer and cook for 15-20 minutes until the sauce has reduced and thickened.

Serve immediately over freshly cooked rice or with naan bread.

# SPICY KOFTAS IN AROMATIC COCONUT SAUCE

This fragrant vegan version of a popular Indian dish combines vegetable koftas (meatballs) in an aromatic tomato and coconut based sauce. The koftas are fried first to give them a crisp outer coating before they are added to the creamy and delicious gravy.

**Preparation Time**
10 minutes

**Total Time**
35 minutes

**Makes**
4 servings

## INGREDIENTS

### FOR THE KOFTAS

8.8oz / 250g zucchini, grated
4.5oz / 125g potatoes, peeled, boiled and mashed
4-5 scallions, finely chopped
1 ½ tbsp chickpeas flour (you can make your own by grinding dried chickpeas in a blender then sieving out larger pieces)
1 tbsp all-purpose flour
½ tbsp garam masala
2 tbsp fresh cilantro leaves, chopped
1 green chili, chopped
½ tsp cumin powder
½ tsp paprika
½ tsp coarse salt
½ tsp freshly ground pepper
3 tbsp vegetable oil

### FOR THE SAUCE

1 tbsp vegetable oil
2 bay leaves
1 cinnamon stick
1 tsp cumin seeds
1 tsp freshly grated ginger
2 garlic cloves, minced
1 tsp turmeric powder
1 tsp red chili powder
2 tsp coriander powder
1 tsp garam masala
1 can chopped tomatoes
1 cup coconut milk
1 tsp lemon juice

# DIRECTIONS

Preheat the oven to 250 °F / 120°c.

In a large skillet heat the oil over low heat. While the oil is heating mix all the kofta ingredients together in a large bowl until well combined.

Shape the koftas into small balls and fry them in batches, making sure to not overcrowd the pan. Each kofta ball will need approx 4-5 minutes to cook and are done when golden brown and crispy on the outside. Remove the cooked koftas with a slotted spoon and transfer to a paper towel lined plate. Continue until all koftas are fried then place in the preheated oven to keep them warm.

To make the sauce heat a large frying pan with oil. Once hot add the bay leaf, cinnamon stick and cumin seeds and stir constantly for 1 minute to flavor the oil. Add garlic, ginger, and the remainder of spices and stir for another minute. Pour in the chopped tomatoes and coconut milk and bring to a boil. Reduce to a simmer and cook for 5 minutes.

Remove the cinnamon stick and bay leaf and very carefully transfer to a blender. Pulse the sauce until very smooth. You may wish to do this in two batches depending on the size of your blender.

Return sauce to the pan and simmer on low for 10 minutes or until the sauce has thickened to your desired consistency. Add the lemon juice and mix.

Remove the koftas from the oven and carefully place in the sauce, coating all sides.

Serve over basmati rice or with naan bread.

# PUMPKIN DAHL SOUP

Pumpkin adds a warm color and beautiful flavor to this hearty dahl soup. The soup is spiced with wonderful Indian flavors and takes only 15 minutes to prepare.

**Preparation Time**
15 minutes

**Total Time**
40 minutes

**Makes**
4 servings

## INGREDIENTS

### FOR THE SOUP

1 tbsp olive or vegetable oil
1 small onion, finely chopped
3 cloves garlic, minced
1-inch fresh ginger, grated
1 ¼ cup split red lentils
6 cups vegetable stock
2 tsp ground turmeric
1 tsp chili powder
1 tsp ground cumin
½ tsp ground coriander
1 small pumpkin, peeled, seeds removed and cut into chunks
¼ cup cilantro, roughly chopped
½ tsp coarse salt
½ tsp freshly ground pepper

### FOR THE ONION TOPPING

2 medium onions, cut into thin slices
2 tbsp olive or vegetable oil
2 small red chilies, chopped
2 cloves garlic, finely chopped

## DIRECTIONS

Heat oil in a medium saucepan. Once hot add onions and saute for 3-4 minutes until softened. Add garlic and ginger and cook for a minute. Add the turmeric, chili powder, cumin and coriander and stir constantly for a minute.

Pour in the stock and lentils and bring to a boil. Reduce heat to a simmer and cook covered for 15 minutes. Add the pumpkin chunks and cook covered for 10 minutes.

While the soup is cooking heat a frying pan with oil. Once hot fry the onions for 3 minutes until brown and tender. Add garlic and chilies and fry for 6-7 minutes over low heat, stirring frequently. Set aside.

Remove the lid from the soup and check the pumpkin is cooked by piercing with a fork. If it is not tender increase heat and boil for 5 minutes until the pumpkin is soft.

Using a soup blender or a food processor puree the soup. Pulse to a smooth or chunky soup depending on your preference. Be very careful during the step as the soup will be extremely hot.

Stir in chopped cilantro and pour into serving bowls.

Evenly garnish with onion topping and serve immediately while hot.

# PALAK TOFU (SPINACH TOFU CURRY)

Palak is a popular North Indian curry made of blanched spinach, and this veganised version features tasty tofu. The creamy and rich sauce comes in the form of cashew nuts which could rival any dairy based version.

**Preparation Time**
15 minutes (+ ½ hour to soak the cashew nuts)

**Total Time**
40 minutes

**Makes**
4 servings

## INGREDIENTS

5 cups fresh spinach, washed
1 cup unsalted raw cashews
1 cup vegetable stock
¾ cup coconut water
12oz / 340g firm tofu, cut into small chunks
1 tbsp vegetable oil
1 tsp curry powder
1 tsp ground paprika
1 tsp ginger powder

1 tsp turmeric
½ tsp cumin powder
1-inch piece fresh ginger, grated
½ cup coconut milk
½ cup tomato purée
1 tsp coarse salt
½ tsp freshly ground black pepper

## DIRECTIONS

Leave the cashew nuts to soften in 1 cup of hot stock for half an hour. Transfer the nuts and stock to a food processor or blender and pulse until very smooth. Add the spinach and coconut water and blend again until smooth. Set aside.

In a large saucepan heat the vegetable oil over medium heat and add the tofu, curry powder, paprika, ginger powder, turmeric and cumin. Cook for 5-6 minutes until soft and fully coated with the spice mixture. Add the grated ginger and fry for a further 1-2 minutes.

Pour the spinach cashew mix over the tofu and add the coconut milk, tomato puree, salt and pepper and mix well. Simmer for 20 minutes, stirring occasionally.

Serve over freshly cooked basmati rice or with naan bread.

# AUTHENTIC SPICED VEGETABLE BIRYANI

This healthy and delicious biryani is made up of vegetables and rice. It is a simple dish that is very versatile, served either as a side or as a main meal. Clean up is easy as the biryani cooks in one big pot.

| **Preparation Time** | **Total Time** | **Makes** |
|---|---|---|
| 15 minutes | 1 hour | 6 servings |

## INGREDIENTS

2 tbsp vegetable oil
1 small cauliflower head, stem removed and cut into small florets
2 large potatoes, washed, peeled and cubed (you can use sweet potatoes if you prefer)
½ tsp coarse salt
½ tsp freshly ground black pepper
1 large onion, chopped
4 ¼ cups vegetable stock
3 tbsp hot curry paste
1 fresh green chili, finely chopped

1 tsp cumin seeds
2 tsp mustard seeds
5-6 cardamom seeds
3-4 whole cloves
2 tsp turmeric
2 ½ cups basmati rice
1 cup fresh or frozen peas
5oz / 150g french long beans, ends removed
2 lemons, freshly squeezed
2 tbsp fresh cilantro leaves, roughly chopped
1/3 cup salted cashew nuts, roasted

## DIRECTIONS

Preheat the oven to 400°F / 200°c.

Place the cauliflower, potatoes and onions in a large ovenproof dish and drizzle with 3 tbsp vegetable oil, salt and pepper and use a spoon ensure vegetables are evenly coated in oil. Bake in the oven for 15 minutes.

While the vegetables are in the oven mix together the stock, hot curry paste, chili, cumin seeds, mustard seeds, cardamom seeds, cloves and turmeric in a large bowl and set aside.

Remove the vegetables from the oven and reduce the temperature to 370°F / 190°c. Mix rice, beans and peas into the par-cooked vegetables. Pour stock mixture over and combine. Cover tightly with foil and carefully pierce a few holes with a fork in order to let some steam out. Bake in the oven for 30 minutes or until the rice is tender and has absorbed all the liquid.

Remove from the oven, stir in lemon juice and cilantro and transfer to a large serving plate. Sprinkle roasted cashew nuts over the top and serve immediately while hot.

# TANDOORI SPICED QUINOA

This Tandoori spiced quinoa was inspired by the popular dish 'Tandoori Chicken' and captures its authentic flavors. This dish is very easy to make as all ingredients cook together in one pot, making cleanup a breeze!

**Preparation Time**
10 minutes

**Total Time**
30 minutes

**Makes**
4-5 servings

## INGREDIENTS

1 tbsp olive oil
1 cup sweet potatoes, peeled and cut into small bite size cubes
½ small onion, finely chopped
2 cloves garlic, minced
2 green chilies, finely chopped
1 tsp fresh ginger, minced
2 tbsp garam masala
½ tsp chili powder
1 tsp cumin powder
1 tsp coriander powder

½ tsp turmeric powder
1 cup quinoa, thoroughly rinsed
1 ½ cup vegetable stock
1 can (14oz / 400g) chickpeas
1 can chopped tomatoes
1 tsp sugar
½ tsp coarse salt
½ tsp freshly ground pepper
1 fresh lime or lemon, cut into wedges
2 tbsp fresh cilantro, roughly chopped

## DIRECTIONS

Heat oil over medium-high heat in a large saucepan. Add the onions and cook for 2-3 minutes. Stir in the sweet potato and fry for around 7-8 minutes until softened. Add the garlic, ginger and fresh chili and cook for 30 seconds, then mix in the garam masala, chili powder, cumin powder, coriander powder and turmeric powder and cook for another 30 seconds until fragrant.

Pour in the chickpeas, chopped tomatoes and stock and bring to a boil. Once the liquid is boiling add the quinoa, salt and pepper and mix well. Cover and reduce the heat to a simmer. Cook for 15 minutes, uncover and cook for a further 5-7 minutes to reduce the liquid.

Remove from the heat, transfer to a large serving bowl and sprinkle with chopped cilantro. Place lemon or lime wedges around the sides of the dish and serve while piping hot.

# COCONUT TOFU 'KEEMA'

A warm, sweet and delicately spiced Indian curry that's easy to make. You can add various different vegetables according to what you have to hand or what is in season.

**Preparation Time**
20 minutes

**Total Time**
1 hour and 5 minutes

**Makes**
4-5 servings

## INGREDIENTS

2 tbsp vegetable or olive oil
4 cloves garlic, minced
½ medium onion, finely chopped
1 tsp cumin powder
1 tsp curry powder
1 tsp paprika
1 tsp ground ginger powder
1 (7oz / 200g) package extra firm tofu, pressed (see below)

1 (14oz / 420g) can coconut milk
6 cups tomato sauce or passata
1 tsp coarse salt
½ tsp freshly ground black pepper
1 cup fresh or frozen peas, thawed
2 large carrots, chopped

## DIRECTIONS

To start, remove tofu from packaging and press between two towels to remove excess water. You can use something weighted, such as a large saucepan or chopping board and place this on top of the tofu to squeeze out as much moisture as possible for a minimum of 10 minutes. This process will allow the tofu to absorb much more flavor. After 10 minutes chop tofu into small cubes. Set aside.

Heat oil in a large frying pan over medium-high heat. Saute the onions for 2-3 minutes then add the garlic, cumin powder, curry powder, paprika, and ginger and stir constantly for 30 seconds.

Add the pressed tofu and cook, covered, for 8-10 minutes over low heat. If the tofu appears to be drying up add a splash of water to the pan.

Pour in coconut milk and tomato sauce and bring to a boil.

Reduce to a low simmer and add carrots, peas and seasoning. Simmer covered for 20 minutes, then uncover and simmer for 10 more minutes to thicken the liquid.

Serve over basmati rice or naan bread.

# BESAN CHEELA
# (EGGLESS VEGETABLE OMELET)

This is a delicious, tender and fluffy omelet that is made using chickpea flour instead of eggs. It's packed full of vegetables, however, it is important to chop them all to the same size so that they cook evenly and you avoid having large chunks of vegetables in the batter.

**Preparation Time**
10 minutes (+ 15 minutes for the batter to rest)

**Total Time**
1 hour and 5 minutes

**Makes**
4-5 servings

## INGREDIENTS

½ cup chickpea or garbanzo bean flour
½ small onion, finely chopped
¼ small tomato, finely chopped
2 button mushrooms, finely chopped
¼ bell pepper, finely chopped (you can use any color you like)
½ tsp fresh ginger, grated

1 large garlic clove, grated
½ tsp chili powder
¼ tsp turmeric
¼ tsp cumin powder
½ tsp salt
¼ tsp freshly ground black pepper
2 tbsp cilantro leaves, chopped
¾ - 1 cup water
2 tbsp vegetable oil, for frying

## DIRECTIONS

Add all ingredients except the water and oil to a large bowl and mix well to combine. Cover and allow to rest for 15 minutes.

Add ¾ cup of water and mix. The batter needs to be slightly thinner than usual pancake batter so add 1 tablespoon at a time of the remaining ¼ cup of water if necessary.

Heat a large frying pan with vegetable oil. Once hot pour half of the batter into the center and move the pan around to spread the mixture around evenly. Cook until the edges of the omelet are no longer wet, then using a spatula quickly flip over to cook on the other side for 1-2 minutes. Repeat with remaining batter.

# ALOO GOBI
# (POTATO & CAULIFLOWER CURRY)

This Punjabi classic is a dry curry made with potatoes, cauliflower and fragrant Indian spices. It is commonly served as a side dish to accompany a main meal.

| **Preparation Time** | **Total Time** | **Makes** |
|---|---|---|
| 15 minutes | 20 minutes | 4 servings |

## INGREDIENTS

2 tbsp vegetable oil
1 medium potato, peeled and cut into 8-10 wedges
1 small cauliflower head, stem removed and cut into small florets
½ cup fresh or frozen peas
1 medium onion, finely chopped
½ tsp fresh ginger, minced
2 garlic cloves, minced
1 small fresh green chili, chopped

1 tsp cumin seeds
1 tsp mustard seeds
½ tsp turmeric powder
½ tsp coriander powder
½ tsp garam masala
½ tsp chili powder
2 tbsp tomato puree
3 tbsp water
2 tbsp fresh cilantro leaves, chopped
½ tsp coarse salt
¼ tsp pepper

## DIRECTIONS

Heat a large pot with oil over medium heat. Once hot add the cumin and mustard seeds, stirring constantly for 30 seconds. Saute the onions for 2-3 minutes then add the ginger, garlic and fresh chili and fry for 1 minute. Add the turmeric, garam masala, coriander powder, and chili powder, and stir constantly for 30 seconds, then add the tomato puree and water and cook for a minute.

Reduce the heat to low then stir in the cauliflower and potatoes, cover and cook for 5 minutes until the vegetables are tender, add the peas, re-cover and cook for 3-4 minutes.

Season with salt and pepper, remove from heat and transfer to a serving bowl.

Garnish with chopped cilantro.

# SIDES

# INDIAN SPICED LEMON RICE

An aromatic basmati rice which has been flavored with cumin, cardamom and lemon along with other Indian flavors. The delicious spicy rice is perfect served alongside your favorite curry.

**Preparation Time**
10 minutes (+ 30 minutes for the rice to stand)

**Total Time**
50 minutes

**Makes**
4 servings

## INGREDIENTS

1 cup Basmati rice
1 small onion, finely chopped
1-2 garlic cloves, finely chopped
2 green chilies, finely chopped (Remove the seeds for less heat)
1-inch fresh ginger, peeled and grated
¼ cup raw cashew nuts, roughly chopped
½ tsp turmeric

1 lemon, juiced
Zest from 1 lemon
2 tsp olive oil
1 tsp cumin seeds
1 tsp mustard seeds
5-6 cardamom pods
1 tsp cloves
½ tsp coarse salt
½ tsp freshly ground black pepper
2 tbsp fresh cilantro, roughly chopped

## DIRECTIONS

Pour rice in a pot and add enough water to just cover it. Leave the rice to stand for 30 minutes then discard the water and give the rice a quick rinse.

Bring just under 2 cups of water and 1 tsp salt to a rolling boil. Add rice, turmeric, cardamon and cloves, reduce heat to a simmer then cover the pot and leave to cook for 20 minutes over low heat.

While the rice is cooking heat a saucepan with 2 tbsp olive oil. Once hot add onions and saute for 2-3 minutes until soft. Add garlic and ginger and cook over medium-low heat for a minute then stir in mustard seeds and cumin seeds. Once the mustard seeds start to pop add chilies and cashew nuts, stirring frequently for 4-5 minutes. Remove from the heat and set aside until the rice has finished cooking.

Add onion-spice mixture to the cooked rice, pour in lemon juice and zest and mix well.

Top with cilantro.

# AROMATIC INFUSED SAFFRON RICE

The secret to this brightly colored aromatic side dish is steeping the saffron in hot water for a few minutes before mixing it into the rice as this helps release the wonderfully distinct flavor of saffron.

**Preparation Time**
5 minutes (+ 30 minutes for the rice to soak)

**Total Time**
25 minutes

**Makes**
6 servings

## INGREDIENTS

14oz / 400g basmati rice, thoroughly washed and soaked for 30 minutes
2 pinches of saffron
2 tbsp vegan butter

1 small white onion, chopped
3 bay leaves
2 cups / 475ml vegetable stock
½ tsp salt

## DIRECTIONS

Place one pinch of saffron in a pestle and mortar and grind it into a powder then add another pinch of saffron threads. Pour ¼ cup of hot water into your pestle and mortar and allow it to sit for 5 minutes. This will help bring the flavor out of the saffron.

Heat butter in a large heavy-bottomed pot over medium heat and once melted add the onion. Saute for 5-6 minutes until soft then add the bay leaves and the rice and stir constantly for a minute. Add the saffron water, using a spatula to ensure there are no remains in the mortar then pour in boiling stock and salt, and mix well.

Bring to a boil then reduce to a low simmer, cover and cook for 15 minutes until the rice is fully cooked and all the liquid has been absorbed.

Remove from the heat and use a fork to fluff the rice up by separating the grains. Remove the bay leaves and serve immediately.

# BOMBAY POTATOES

This simple, easy to follow recipe consists of hearty potatoes combined with beautiful and aromatic Indian flavors and makes a delicious side dish.

**Preparation Time**
20 minutes

**Total Time**
55 minutes

**Makes**
4 servings

## INGREDIENTS

1.5 lbs / 680g new potatoes
1-inch fresh ginger, peeled and grated
3 garlic cloves, minced
2 large ripe tomatoes
1 tbsp tomato puree
½ tbsp olive or vegetable oil
1 tsp cumin seeds
1 tsp mustard seeds
1 fresh green chili, deseeded and chopped
1 small red onion, finely chopped

½ tsp turmeric
1 tsp ground cumin
1 tsp garam masala
1 tsp ground coriander
½ tsp chili powder
½ tsp coarse salt
½ tsp freshly ground black pepper
3-4 scallions sliced
2 tbsp fresh cilantro, roughly chopped

## DIRECTIONS

Place the potatoes in a large saucepan and fill with water until just covered. Bring the water to a boil and cook potatoes for 6-7 minutes until just tender but not fully cooked.

Drain water and set aside to cool down. Once the potatoes have cooled cut them in half.

Place ginger, garlic, tomato puree and 1 roughly chopped tomato in a blender and pulse until smooth. Set aside.

Heat oil in a skillet over medium heat and add cumin and

mustard seeds. Once the mustard seeds start to pop after around 1 minute add the onions and saute for 2-3 minutes. Add chili and cook for a minute.

Spoon in the ginger garlic mixture along with the turmeric, cumin, garam masala, ground coriander and chili powder. Saute over low heat for a minute or two. While the spices are cooking cut the last tomato into wedges and remove the seeds.

Add the tomato and halved potatoes and mix well to combine. Cook for 5 minutes then add the scallions and fry for a minute.

Transfer to a large serving bowl and garnish with fresh cilantro.

# SPICY CURRY FRIES WITH CUCUMBER & MINT RAITA

These golden crispy fries are covered in wonderful Indian spices and served with a cool and refreshing mint raita, which has been made using tofu to recreate the creamy texture of yoghurt.

**Preparation Time**
10 minutes

**Total Time**
50 minutes

**Makes**
4 servings

## INGREDIENTS

FOR THE HOT CURRY FRIES

2 large russet potatoes, washed and scrubbed
3 tbsp olive or vegetable oil
1 tbsp all-purpose flour
1 heaped tbsp corn flour
1½ tbsp Madras curry powder
1 tsp paprika
1 tsp coarse salt

FOR THE CUCUMBER MINT RAITA

12oz / 340g silken tofu
2 tbsp lemon juice
1 medium cucumber, cut into 2-inch chunks
¼ cup fresh mint leaves, roughly chopped
2 tbsp fresh cilantro leaves, roughly chopped
½ tsp ground cumin
¼ tsp coarse salt

## DIRECTIONS

TO MAKE THE HOT CURRY FRIES:

Preheat the oven to 430°F / 220°c. Line a baking tray with parchment paper.

Cut potatoes into ¼ inch thick sticks and pat dry with a paper towel to remove any excess moisture.

In a large bowl add oil, cornstarch, flour, curry powder and paprika and mix well. Add potatoes and stir to coat each potato stick.

Arrange the potatoes in a single layer on the baking tray (you may need to use two trays depending on how large your oven is) and bake in the oven for 25-30 minutes.

Turn the chips 2-3 times during cooking to ensure all sides are golden brown.

While the chips are baking in the oven you can make the raita.

Place tofu and lemon juice in a food processor and blend until completely smooth, stopping to scraping down the sides a few times as you go along. Add the cucumber, mint, cilantro, cumin and salt and pulse in short bursts until the cucumber is finely chopped and all ingredients are well combined.

Transfer to a serving bowl.

# RESTAURANT–STYLE GARLIC NAAN

No Indian meal is complete without the addition of a soft pillowy piece of naan to mop up all the wonderfully spiced sauces common to Indian cuisine. This aromatic garlic infused naan is made on the stove and makes the perfect accompaniment to an Indian main meal.

**Preparation Time**
10 minutes (+ 1 ½ hours for the dough to prove)

**Total Time**
30 minutes

**Makes**
6 pieces of naan bread

## INGREDIENTS

1 tsp active dry yeast
½ cup warm water (between 105-110°c)
3 tbsp dairy free milk
2 tbsp vegetable oil
½ tbsp sugar
1 tsp salt
½ tsp onion powder

½ tsp garlic powder
1 ¾ cup strong flour
2 cloves garlic, finely chopped
1 tbsp vegan butter
2 tbsp parsley, chopped
1 tsp chili flakes

## DIRECTIONS

In a large bowl stir the yeast into the warm water and leave it to activate for 10 minutes until it develops 'froth' on the surface. If froth does not appear then your yeast needs to be replaced.

Mix in the dairy free milk, oil, sugar, salt, onion powder, and garlic powder. Slowly add the flour with a wooden spoon until you have a rough dough. Transfer to a lightly floured surface and knead for up to 10 minutes until you have a soft dough.

Pour 1 tablespoon of oil in a large bowl and use your palm

to cover the inside surface. Place the dough inside and roll it around so that it is lightly coated in oil. Cover with plastic wrap and allow the dough to rise for 1 hour until it doubles in size.

Once it has risen punch the dough a few times to release some air then roll it into 6 evenly sized balls and place these directly on parchment paper. Cover with plastic wrap and let them rest again for 30 minutes.

After the second proving preheat a pan over medium heat with a little olive oil. Roll each ball into an oval shape and once the pan is hot fry one naan at a time for 2-3 minutes then flip them over and fry again for another 2-3 minutes until it has puffed up and slightly browned on the surface. Remove, brush with a little butter and sprinkle with parsley and chili flakes. Repeat with remaining dough.

# SPICED POTATO & PEA PARATHAS

This whole wheat Indian flatbread is a recipe you will be making over and over again. The soft yet crisp paratha is stuffed with mashed potatoes, peas and flavored with garlic, chilies and cumin. A wonderful side dish, appetizer or snack.

**Preparation Time**
40 minutes (+ 2 hours for dough to rest)

**Total Time**
1 hour and 10 minutes

**Makes**
8 parathas / Serves 4-8

## INGREDIENTS

FOR THE PARATHA DOUGH

1 cup whole wheat flour
1 cup all-purpose flour
1 tsp coarse salt
1 cup lukewarm water
2 tbsp vegetable oil

FOR THE POTATO FILLING

1 lb / ½ kg Yukon Gold or Rooster potatoes, washed, scrubbed and cut into 1-inch chunks
2 tbsp vegetable oil

½ tsp mustard seeds
½ tsp cumin seeds
1 tsp turmeric
2-3 garlic cloves, crushed
1 medium onion, finely chopped
2 fresh green chilies, seeded and chopped
1 cup peas, fresh or frozen
1 tsp salt
½ tsp freshly ground black pepper
2 tbsp cilantro leaves

## DIRECTIONS

In a large bowl mix whole wheat, all-purpose flour and salt together. Using a wooden spoon slowly add water and mix well until a sticky dough forms.

Sprinkle flour onto a clean work surface and knead the dough using your hands for around 5 minutes, punching the center with your fist and pulling the dough back into the center. Place dough back into the bowl, cover with plastic wrap and leave to rest at room temperature for 2 hours.

While the dough is resting you can make the potato filling. Place the cubed potatoes into a pot and fill with just enough water to cover. Bring to a boil and cook for around 15 minutes or until tender when pierced with a fork. Drain and discard the water and using a fork or potato masher roughly crush the potatoes so that it turns to a very chunky mash. Set aside.

In a large skillet heat oil over medium heat. Once hot add mustard and cumin seeds and fry for around 1 minute or until the seeds start to pop. Add onions and saute for 2-3 minutes until soft and tender then stir in turmeric and garlic. Fry for 5 minutes and add chilies, mixing well.

Stir in the potatoes and peas and cook for 2-3 minutes, then add chopped cilantro and seasoning.

After 2 hours remove the dough from the bowl and using a knife split into 8 even sized balls. Roll each piece of dough into an 8-inch round disk and spoon approx. 3-4 tablespoons of the potato filling onto one half of the disk only and spread it evenly. Fold the dough in half so that you have covered the filling and then fold it over once more into a quarter.

Roll the filled dough out again so that you have flattened the filling. You can add some flour to the rolling pin to prevent it from cracking, however, do not worry if it breaks a little. Repeat with the remaining dough and filling.

Heat vegetable oil in a large frying pan over medium-high heat. Add the paratha to the pan once hot and cook for 2-3 minutes, flipping over after 1 minute of cooking. The paratha should be golden brown on both sides. Remove from heat and transfer to a paper towel lined plate. Repeat with remaining parathas.

# SPICY TIKKA BITES

Tikka bites are a common street food in India and this recipe recreates the authentic taste and texture while keeping it 100% vegan. Tikka bites are beautifully golden and crispy fried balls of potato, cabbage and onion spiced to perfection.

| **Preparation Time** | **Total Time** | **Makes** |
| 5 minutes (+ 1 hour for mixture to chill in fridge) | 15 minutes | 4 servings |

## INGREDIENTS

4 medium potatoes, washed and peeled
1 tsp coarse salt, divided
1 cup red cabbage, grated (approx ¼ head)
1 medium onion, finely chopped
2 garlic cloves, minced
1 small green chili, finely chopped

1 tsp chili powder
½ tsp coriander seeds
1 tsp cumin seeds
½ tsp garam masala powder
2 tbsp fresh cilantro, chopped
2 tbsp freshly squeezed lemon juice
Vegetable oil

## DIRECTIONS

Place potatoes and ½ tsp salt in a medium saucepan and fill with enough water to just cover them. Bring water to a boil and cook for around 15 minutes or until the potatoes are tender when pierced with a fork. Once cooked drain and discard the water and leave to cool for a few minutes. Once cool enough to touch roughly chop the potatoes.

While the potatoes are cooking heat 1 tbsp oil in a frying pan and once hot add coriander and cumin seeds. Fry for 1 minute until fragrant. Add onions and fry for 2-3 minutes, then add garlic and fresh chili, cooking for a minute. Add chili powder and garam masala and fry for another minute. Mix in cabbage and fry for around 5 minutes until tender then remove from heat and transfer to a large mixing bowl.

Add the cooked and chopped potatoes to the onion mixture along with the cilantro and lemon juice. Mash very well using a potato masher, a fork or even your hands. Cover with plastic wrap and chill in the fridge for 1 hour.

Remove mixture from fridge and form 8-10 equal sized round balls- then flatten each one slightly in the palm of your hands. Heat a pan with 4-5 tablespoons of vegetable oil over medium-high heat. Once the oil is hot fry the balls in batches (you can test this by dropping a tiny piece of the potato mixture in - if it rises to the top and sizzles immediately it is ready). Make sure not to overcrowd the pan or it will prevent the tikka bits from getting crispy.

Fry each ball for 2-3 minutes until golden and crisp on the outside. Remove with a slotted spoon and transfer to a paper towel lined plate.

Serve immediately while hot and crispy with chutney or a sauce of your choice.

# CRISPY ZUCCHINI BHAJIS

A unique take on onion bhajis that have been oven baked instead of fried- making them light, fluffy and healthy. They freeze well - you simply need to defrost the bhajis and pop them in the oven for 6-7 minutes to reheat.

**Preparation Time**
15 minutes (+20 minutes to draw out water from the zucchinis)

**Total Time**
35 minutes

**Makes**
8-10 bhajis / Serves 3-4 as a side

## INGREDIENTS

1.3 lbs / 600g zucchinis, washed and grated
1 ½ tbsp vegetable oil, divided
1 tsp curry powder
½ tsp cumin seeds
½ tsp turmeric powder
1 large onion, finely chopped
1 fresh red chili, finely chopped,
2 garlic cloves, minced
1 tsp freshly grated ginger
1 tbsp cornstarch

¼ tsp baking powder
¼ cup water
1/3 cup unsweetened non-dairy milk, soy, coconut or almond
1 cup + 1 tbsp gram flour (also known as chickpea flour or garbanzo bean flour)
1 ¾ tsp baking powder, divided
1 ½ tsp coarse salt, divided
Freshly ground black pepper

## DIRECTIONS

Place the grated zucchini in a sieve and sprinkle with 1 tsp salt, then mix well and massage with your hands to coat. Leave the zucchini in the sieve for 20 minutes in order to remove excess water. This will prevent the bhajis from becoming soggy and enable them to crisp up.

After 20 minutes rinse under water to remove the salt then squeeze handfuls of the grated zucchini in order to ring out as much liquid as possible. Spread out on a cloth once you have removed the liquid from each handful. Place another cloth on top and press down to remove as much water as possible.

Transfer to a medium sized bowl and use a fork to separate it. Set aside.

Preheat the oven to 390°F / 200°c. Line a baking tray with parchment paper and lightly grease with a little oil.

Heat a frying pan with ½ tbsp vegetable oil and once hot fry the cumin seeds for 30 seconds, then add the curry powder, frying for a further 30 seconds. Fry the onions for 2-3 minutes then finally add the garlic, ginger and chili, cooking for 30 seconds. Remove from the heat and set aside.

In a small bowl whisk together the cornstarch, ¼ tsp baking powder and turmeric. In a separate bowl mix ¼ cup water and 1 tbsp vegetable oil. Slowly add the wet ingredients to the dry and whisk well, for a minute or two, until you have a very thick mixture. Slowly add the non-dairy milk a tablespoon at a time and continue to whisk well after each addition. You need to continually whisk in order to prevent the mixture from becoming too thin.

In a medium bowl add the gram flour, ½ tsp salt and 1½ tsp baking powder and mix to combine. Add the grated zucchini, the cornstarch mixture and the fried onions and stir very well using a fork until fully combined and the mixture is thick.

Drop heaped tablespoons of the mixture onto the baking sheet and gently shape using the spoon. Continue with remaining mixture. Bake in the preheated oven for 15-17 minutes or until they are golden brown and fully cooked inside.

Serve with chutney or a sauce of your choice.

# ALOO TIKKI

This authentic and exotic snack or side dish consists of mashed potato, peas and wonderfully fragrant spices which are fried to create a crisp golden exterior and a warm fluffy inner crust. These are perfect served with your favorite chutney.

**Preparation Time**
10 minutes

**Total Time**
20 minutes

**Makes**
8 large patties /
serves 4 as a side

## INGREDIENTS

3 large white potatoes, peeled
½ tsp salt
¾ cup fresh or frozen peas
½ red onion, finely chopped
1 green chili, finely chopped
1 tsp chili powder
2 tsp garam masala
1 tsp cumin powder
1 tsp coriander powder

1 garlic clove, minced
1 tbsp fresh ginger, grated
1 handful fresh parsley leaves, roughly chopped
2 tbsp bread crumbs
4 tbsp flour
½ tsp baking powder
½ tsp salt
½ tsp pepper

## DIRECTIONS

Place potatoes and ½ tsp salt in a saucepan and fill with enough water to just cover. Bring to a boil and cook for 10-15 minutes until the potatoes are tender when pierced with a fork. Once cooked drain and discard the water, transfer the potatoes back into the saucepan and mash using a potato masher or a fork until smooth and lump-free.

Transfer the mashed potatoes into a large mixing bowl and add chili, chili powder, garam masala, cumin powder, coriander powder, garlic clove, ginger, parsley leaves, breadcrumbs, flour, baking powder, salt and pepper. Mix very well until all ingredients are well combined.

Form 8 equal sized patties and place on a clean surface or chopping board.

Heat oil over medium-high heat and once hot fry each patty for 2-3 minutes, flipping halfway through cooking, until golden brown. Fry the patties in batches as you do not want to overcrowd the pan. Remove cooked patty with a slotted spoon and transfer to a paper towel lined plate.

Serve immediately while hot with chutney or your favorite dipping sauce.

# CRISPY ONION PAKORAS

A popular street food most commonly served on the streets of Mumbai. This appetiser, snack or side dish is made with chickpea flour and an array of wonderful Indian spices.

**Preparation Time**
5 minutes (+ 10 minutes for the batter to rest)

**Total Time**
25 minutes

**Makes**
4 servings

## INGREDIENTS

2 medium onions, thinly sliced, lengthways
¾ cup chickpea flour (also known as gram or besan flour)
¼ tsp baking powder
½ cup water
½ tsp turmeric powder

1 tsp cumin seeds
½ tsp black mustard seeds
¼ cup fresh cilantro leaves
1 tsp fresh ginger, grated
1 small green chili, finely chopped
Oil, for frying (Vegetable or Canola)

## DIRECTIONS

Place sliced onions in a large mixing bowl. In a separate bowl combine all ingredients except the water and oil, being sure to mix well. Add ½ cup of water very slowly, whisking after each addition. The batter should be thick and of a similar consistency to yogurt.

Add the batter to the onions and mix well to coat all slices. Cover with plastic wrap and leave to rest for 10 minutes.

Heat around 2-inches of oil in a pan over medium-high heat. To test whether the oil is hot enough to fry the onions, drop a small piece of onion in, if it rises to the surface and sizzles it is ready. If you have a kitchen thermometer the oil needs to be 340°F /

170°c.

Once the oil is hot enough drop a heaped tablespoon of the onion batter into the pan. Cook for a 1 ½ minutes on each side, 3 minutes in total for each pakora. You should be able to fry a few pakora at the same time, but make sure you don't overcrowd the pan or they will not crisp up. They are ready when they are cooked throughout and the exterior is golden brown and crispy.

Remove each pakora from the pan using a slotted spoon and transfer to a paper towel lined plate.

# HARA BHARA KABAB
## (VEGETABLE CUTLETS)

A delectable combination of mashed potato and green vegetables, which are crisp on the outside, and soft and fluffy on the inside. These Indian potato kebabs are simple to make and can be served as an appetiser, a snack or a side dish.

**Preparation Time**
20 minutes

**Total Time**
30 minutes

**Makes**
20 kebabs / Serves 4

## INGREDIENTS

6 cups fresh spinach, stems removed, washed and finely chopped
14oz / 400g potatoes (Russet or Maris Piper work best)
2 tsp vegetable oil
½ tsp cumin seeds
1 tsp fresh ginger, finely chopped
1 garlic clove, finely chopped

1 ¼ tsp coarse salt, divided
½ tsp freshly ground black pepper
3 tbsp cornstarch
¼ cup coriander, finely chopped
2 tbsp fresh green chili, finely chopped
Vegetable oil, for frying

## DIRECTIONS

Place potatoes and ½ tsp salt in a saucepan and fill with enough water to just cover. Bring to a boil and cook for 10-15 minutes until the potatoes are tender when pierced with a fork. Once cooked drain and discard the water. Peel the potatoes then shred them using a grater. You will need 1 ½ cups of grated potatoes. Set aside.

Heat 2 tsp vegetable oil in a frying pan over medium-high heat. After around 30 seconds add the cumin seeds and cook until they start to crackle. Add the garlic and ginger and fry for 30 seconds, then add the spinach and stir frequently, pressing down as you go along to allow some of the water to evaporate. Remove from the heat and set aside to cool down.

Once the spinach is at room temperature transfer to a large mixing bowl. Using your hands, mix in the grated potatoes, ¾ tsp salt, black pepper, cornstarch, coriander and the fresh green chili to form a soft dough.

Divide the dough into 20 equal parts and roll each part into an oval sausage-like shape.

Heat 1-inch of oil in a frying pan over medium-high heat and wait for it to get hot. To test whether the oil is hot enough to fry the kebabs drop a small piece of dough in, if it rises to the surface and sizzles it is ready. If you have a kitchen thermometer the oil needs to be 340°F / 170°c.

Fry the kebabs for around 6-7 minutes, ensuring each side is evenly cooked. You will need to fry them in batches as you do not want to overcrowd the pan. This will prevent them from becoming crispy.

Remove each kebab with a slotted spoon and transfer to a paper towel lined plate.

Serve immediately while hot and crispy with a chutney of your choice.

# INDIAN SWEETS

# BESAN HALWA

This traditional Punjabi dessert made with chickpea flour is soft, sweet and fudgy, and comes together within 20 minutes - making it the perfect Indian treaty to curb a sweet tooth.

**Preparation Time**
5 minutes

**Total Time**
20 minutes

**Makes**
2 servings

## INGREDIENTS

3 tbsp coconut oil, melted
¾ cup chickpea flour, sieved
¼ tsp ground cardamom or 1 cardamom pod, crushed in a pestle and mortar
1/3 cup coconut sugar or brown sugar

⅛ tsp salt
¾ cup dairy free milk, warmed
2 tbsp pistachios

## DIRECTIONS

Heat coconut oil in a skillet over medium heat then add chickpea flour and roast over a low heat, stirring frequently until it starts to become a light golden brown and resemble coarse breadcrumbs. Heat the milk in the microwave until warm when you poke your finger in, but not uncomfortably hot. Add the cardamom, salt, and sugar to the warm milk and mix well. Slowly pour in the milk, ¼ cup at a time, and stir constantly to prevent lumps from forming.

Add the nuts and continue to stir for a minute over a low heat to break up any lumps that may form. Remove from the heat and serve immediately.

To store, ensure it has cooled to room temperature then keep in an airtight container in the fridge for 3-4 days.

# COCONUT ALMOND BURFI

A traditional Indian sweet made of coconut, almonds and a subtle hint of cardamom. It is surprisingly easy to make and keeps in the fridge for up to two weeks,

| **Preparation Time** | **Total Time** | **Makes** |
|---|---|---|
| 5 minutes | 25 minutes (+ 1 hour 20 minutes to cool) | 6 servings |

## INGREDIENTS

2 cups desiccated coconut
¾ cup white sugar
½ cup blanched almond powder*

¼ tsp cardamom powder
1 tsp vanilla extract
1 tbsp coconut oil, melted

## DIRECTIONS

*If you are unable to find blanched almond powder in the store you can make your own. Either find blanched almonds or take 1 cup of almonds and soak in boiling water for 10-15 minutes. Drain water and pop the skin off each almond. Leave to dry thoroughly for up to an hour then place in a food processor and pulse in short bursts until a fine powder forms. Be careful not to blend for too long or the almonds will turn to a paste.

Grease a medium sized square dish with a little coconut oil.

Heat a nonstick frying pan for around 30 seconds over medium-low heat. Add the desiccated coconut and sugar and cook for a few minutes until the sugar has completely melted and the mixture starts to simmer.

Slowly mix in the almond powder, vanilla and cardamom and cook for around 7 minutes until the mixture becomes the consistency of a thick dough. You will need to stir the mixture very frequently to prevent it from sticking to the bottom and to ensure it is cooking evenly.

Remove from the heat and pour into greased dish, spreading evenly and pressing down with a spatula. Leave to cool down for 15 minutes then cut into 1-inch squares.

Leave to cool at room temperature for 1 hour then remove burfi from the dish.

The burfi can be kept for up to 2 weeks in an airtight container in the fridge.

# BROWN RICE KHEER

A different take on a classic Indian dessert which is similar to a sweet and creamy rice pudding. Although the dish is traditionally prepared with white rice, brown is not only healthier but has a slightly nutty taste and fuller texture. It does take a little longer to cook than the traditional versions, however, it really is worth the extra time!

**Preparation Time**
10 minutes (+1 hour to soak the rice)

**Total Time**
50 minutes

**Makes**
2 servings

## INGREDIENTS

½ cup brown basmati rice (washed, soaked for 1 hour, then drained)
4 cups / 500ml dairy free milk
2 heaped tbsp sugar
3 cardamoms, seeds

removed and crushed or ½ tsp cardamom powder
Pinch of saffron (optional)
2 to 3 tbsp unsalted pistachios, chopped
3 tbsp golden raisins

## DIRECTIONS

Place milk in a medium saucepan the pour in the rice, keep the flame low so it is barely simmering (or the milk may curdle), cover and cook for 30-40 minutes or until the rice is fully cooked and tender. Stir the rice every 15-20 minutes to prevent it from burning.

Remove from the heat and add sugar and cardamom, stirring constantly. Taste and add more sugar if necessary.

Top with pistachios and raisins.

Serve immediately while hot.

# SWEET POTATO RAS MALAI

A soft and creamy Bengali dessert that consists of sweet dumpling-like balls that act as a sponge to soak up the wonderfully rich and creamy sweet sauce. The traditional version is full of milk and cream, however, we have created this tried and tested version perfectly suitable for vegans! You will need to make the cream sauce one day ahead for the flavors to really intensify.

**Preparation Time**
10 minutes (+1 day for cream sauce flavors to marry)

**Total Time**
35 minutes

**Makes**
4 servings

## INGREDIENTS

### FOR THE RAS MALAI BALLS

1 cup sweet potato, peeled and cubed
½ cup + 1 tbsp almond meal
2 tbsp tapioca starch
1 tsp freshly squeezed lemon juice
1 cardamom pod, peeled and seeds crushed into a powder
1 tbsp sugar or sweetener

### FOR THE RAS (CREAMY SAUCE)

½ cup raw unsalted cashews
½ cup raw unsalted pistachios
2 cardamom pods, gently crushed so the shell has just broken
1 cup dairy free milk
2 tbsp sugar or sweetener
Pinch of saffron (optional)

## DIRECTIONS

TO MAKE THE RAS SAUCE:

Place all sauce ingredients in a bowl, give it a good mix then leave it in the fridge overnight.

TO MAKE THE RAS MAIALI BALLS:

Place sweet potatoes in a saucepan and cover with water. Heat gently until the potatoes are tender when pierced with a fork then remove, drain well and pat dry as much excess moisture as possible.

Transfer the potatoes to a bowl and mash thoroughly until completely smooth and no lumps remain.

Add the almond meal, tapioca, lemon, cardamom powder, and sugar and mix well until fully combined. Shape the mixture into small round dumpling shaped balls and set aside

Turn your steamer on (or boil water in order to create a steamer over a saucepan). Place the Rasmalai balls in the steamer and steam for 5-10 minutes. Remove and place on a plate then prick the balls with a toothpick to allow more of the sauce to be absorbed.

While the balls are steaming remove the sauce from the fridge, discard the cardamom and place in a blender until it becomes smooth and creamy. Transfer to a saucepan and gently heat until it starts to thicken then add the Rasmalai balls, turning them over very gently so both sides are coated in the sauce. Remove from the heat and leave to cool down for an hour or two as this dish is best served cold.

# CLASSIC INDIAN JALEBi

Jalebis are sweet, sticky and syrupy spirals that have been fried to crispy perfection. They are traditionally prepared during festivals in India, however, with this wonderful recipe you can enjoy this delicious sweet treat all year round.

**Preparation Time**
20 minutes (+ 1 hour for the dough to rest)

**Total Time**
1 hour 30 minutes

**Makes**
4 servings

## INGREDIENTS

**FOR THE JALEBI**

4 tbsp sugar
2 cups lukewarm water
1 cup all purpose flour, sieved
1 tbsp vegan yoghurt

**FOR THE SYRUP**

1 ½ cups sugar
1 ½ cups water
2 cardamom seeds, seeds removed and crushed into a powder
Pinch of saffron (optional)

## DIRECTIONS

FOR THE SYRUP

Bring the water to a boil in a medium saucepan. Once boiling add the sugar, cardamom, and saffron. Continue to boil until the mixture has thickened and turned into a thick syrup, around 10-15 minutes. Remove from the heat and set aside.

TO MAKE THE JALEBI

In a large mixing bowl add sugar and water. Mix well for a few minutes until the sugar has dissolved. Add the flour and yoghurt and mix well until the mixture is smooth and no lumps remain. Cover the bowl with a kitchen towel and set aside to rest for 1-2 hours.

Once the dough has rested heat vegetable or canola oil in a large pan until it reaches around 350°F.

A piping bag is the easiest way to create the traditional jalebi shape. Use a 4mm nozzle and transfer the batter into the bag. Pipe the dough in spiral circles directly into the hot oil, and cross the circle to ensure the spiral stays together when removed. You can fry around 3-4 jalebis at the same time. Fry until light golden brown on both sides, around 1-2 minutes.

Remove from the oil using a slotted spoon and place on a paper towel lined plate then continue with the remaining mixture. Once some of the oil had drained place the jalebis into the syrup and ensure both sides are coated. Allow them to absorb the syrup for a minute or two before serving.

Serve immediately while hot.

The jalebis will keep for 2-3 days in a sealed container in the fridge but are best on the day they were fried as it is unlikely that they will stay crisp.

# DATE & NUT LADOOS

These simple and healthy ladoos do not require any sweeteners and can be ready in just 10 minutes. The dates provide a great source of fibre and the nuts are filled with protein. They keep in the fridge for 3 weeks and make a healthy snack to keep on hand.

**Preparation Time**
5 minutes

**Total Time**
10 minutes

**Makes**
18 ladood

## INGREDIENTS

1 cup pitted dates, chopped
1 ½ cups nuts, lightly roasted and roughly chopped (you can use a mixture of different nuts e.g. pecans, pistachios, cashews etc)
2 tbsp cocoa powder

½ tsp instant coffee
¼ tsp cardamom powder (optional)
⅛ tsp coarse salt
2-3 tbsp desiccated coconut
½ tsp vegetable oil

## DIRECTIONS

Place the dates in a small microwave proof bowl and soften in the microwave for 30 seconds.

Transfer to a food processor and pulse until the dates become a paste. Add the instant coffee granules, cocoa powder, cardamom and salt and continue to blend until fully combined. Scrape down the sides with a spatula as you go along.

Add the nuts and blend for another 10-15 seconds but do not over mix as you want the nuts to retain a chunky texture.

Remove the dough from the food processor and place onto a clean surface. Grease the palms of your hands with the vegetable oil and knead the dough for a minute.

Divide the mixture into 18 equally sized balls and roll each ball lightly into the desiccated coconut. Place on a large plate. You can either serve immediately or cover with film and store in the fridge.

The ladoos will keep for up to 3 weeks in an airtight container in the fridge.

# WARM TURMERIC & CINNAMON MILK

This warm and golden milk is spiced with turmeric, ginger, cinnamon and cardamom. It is a traditional drink in India and comes with a huge array of health benefits, as well as being a great aid for sleep.

**Preparation Time**
2 minutes

**Total Time**
6 minutes

**Makes**
2 servings

## INGREDIENTS

2 cups unsweetened almond, coconut, or soy milk
1 tbsp maple syrup
½ tsp ground turmeric
½ tsp ginger

½ tsp cinnamon
½ tsp cardamom
⅛ tsp freshly ground black pepper
1 cinnamon sticks

## DIRECTIONS

In a small saucepan slowly heat the milk over low heat. Once it starts to simmer remove from the heat and add maple syrup and all the spices. Use a whisk to combine well.

Pour into two cups and stir with a cinnamon stick.

Serve while hot.

# MANGO LASSI

Mango Lassi is a 'mango milkshake' usually made with yoghurt, however, this non-dairy version uses blanched almonds and non-dairy milk to replicate the smooth and creamy texture. You can replace the mango with other fruits for a refreshing and healthy drink.

| **Preparation Time** | **Total Time** | **Makes** |
|---|---|---|
| 2 minutes (+ overnight for almonds to soak) | 5 minutes | 2 servings |

## INGREDIENTS

1 cup unsalted blanched almonds, soaked overnight in water
2 cups almond, coconut or soy milk

2 ripe mangoes, peeled and roughly chopped
3 dates
1 tbsp maple syrup
1 tbsp cardamom powder

## DIRECTIONS

Drain almonds and discard water.

Place all ingredients in a blender or food processor and pulse until smooth and creamy.

Pour into a glass over ice if you wish and serve.

# CHUTNEYS

# CORIANDER CHUTNEY

**Preparation Time**
5 minutes

**Total Time**
5 minutes

**Makes**
around ¾ cup
chutney

## INGREDIENTS

1 large bunch of coriander, roughly chopped
3 green chilies, chopped
3 tbsp freshly squeezed lemon juice
1 large garlic clove
½ inch ginger

¾ tsp coarse salt
½ tsp freshly ground black pepper
1 tsp cumin seeds
1 tsp vegetable oil
½ tsp white sugar

## DIRECTIONS

Add all ingredients, except coriander, into a food processor and pulse until a smooth paste forms. Slowly add coriander, a handful at a time and continue to blend until smooth. Add 1 tbsp water at a time until the desired consistency is reached. The chutney should be thick.

Store in an airtight container for up to 3 days. The chutney also freezes well. Pour into an ice cubes tray and once frozen transfer to a ziplock freezer bag. Freeze for up to 3 months.

# SWEET TAMARIND CHUTNEY

**Preparation Time**
5 minutes

**Total Time**
10 minutes

**Makes**
4 servings

## INGREDIENTS

2 tsp vegetable oil
½ tsp cumin powder
½ tsp cardamom powder
⅛ tsp cinnamon powder

½ tsp ground ginger powder
½ cup tamarind paste
½ cup brown sugar
¾ cup water

## DIRECTIONS

Heat a dry frying pan over medium heat for 30 seconds or so. Add the cumin, cardamom, ginger and cinnamon powder, reduce the heat to medium-low and fry for a minute until fragrant. Add the tamarind paste, sugar and water and stir to combine.

Bring mixture to a boil then reduce and simmer for 2-3 minutes until the sauce has thickened.

Remove from heat, place in a serving bowl and leave to cool to room temperature.

To store place in an airtight container and keep in the fridge for up to 3 days. Allow the chutney to come back to room temperature before serving.

# CARROT & GINGER CHUTNEY

**Preparation Time**
5 minutes

**Total Time**
5 minutes

**Makes**
1 cup of chutney

## INGREDIENTS

2 cups grated carrot
4 garlic cloves, finely
chopped
2 tsp chili powder
½ tsp cumin powder

1 tsp freshly squeezed lemon
2 tsp vegetable oil
½ tsp coarse salt
¼ tsp pepper
2 tbsp water

## DIRECTIONS

Add all ingredients to a food processor or blender and pulse in short bursts, being sure to retain a chunky texture- you do not want a puree.

The chutney will keep for up to 5 days in an airtight container in the fridge.

The chutney will keep for up to 3 days in an airtight container in the fridge.

# GARLIC TOMATO CHUTNEY

**Preparation Time**
5 minutes (+ 10 minutes for the chili to soak)

**Total Time**
15 minutes

**Makes**
¾ cup of chutney

## INGREDIENTS

6 large garlic cloves, finely chopped
½ tsp freshly grated ginger
1 cup tomatoes, finely chopped
2 large dried red chilies, soaked in ¼ cup water for 10 minutes

4 scallions (white part), chopped
1 tbsp coriander, finely chopped
1 tsp olive oil
¼ tsp coarse salt

## DIRECTIONS

Drain the dried chilis, pat dry and finely chop.

Heat olive oil in a frying pan over medium-low heat and add the scallions, ginger and garlic, stirring constantly for 1 minute. Add the chilis and salt and fry for another minute.

Pour in the chopped tomatoes and cook over a low heat for around 10 minutes, stirring frequently, until the tomatoes are soft and tender.

Remove from the heat and allow to cool to room temperature.

In a large bowl add the tomato-scallion mixture and coriander and mix well, mashing the tomatoes a little using a fork.

Store in an airtight container in the fridge for up to 3 days.

# APPLE CHUTNEY

**Preparation Time**
10 minutes

**Total Time**
20 minutes

**Makes**
2 cups of chutney

## INGREDIENTS

2 tbsp fresh ginger, grated
3 tbsp vegan butter or olive oil
4 green chilies, finely chopped
1 kg apples, peeled and grated

½ tsp salt
2 cups sugar
1 tsp turmeric powder
1 tbsp ground cinnamon
½ tbsp nutmeg powder
3 tbsp lemon juice

## DIRECTIONS

Heat butter or oil in a large frying pan over medium-low heat and fry ginger for 1 minute.

Add the chilis and saute for 30 seconds.

Add the apple, sugar, salt and turmeric and cook for 5-6 minute or until the apple is soft and tender.

Stir in the cinnamon and nutmeg and fry for a minute until the spices become fragrant.

Remove from the heat and stir in the lemon juice.

Allow to cool to room temperature before serving.

# COCONUT CHUTNEY

**Preparation Time**
10 minutes

**Total Time**
20 minutes

**Makes**
2 cups of chutney

## INGREDIENTS

1 cup desiccated coconut
3 fresh small red chilies
1-inch piece of tamarind
4-5 medium garlic cloves

1 tsp sugar
½ tsp salt
1-2 tbsp water

## DIRECTIONS

Pulse all ingredients together in a food processor. Blend according to how smooth or chunky you prefer your chutney.

The chutney will keep for 3 days in an airtight container in the fridge.

# MORE GREAT TITLES

## HIGH CEDAR PRESS

## CHECK OUT THE FULL COLLECTION!

CPSIA information can be obtained
at www.ICGtesting.com
Printed in the USA
BVHW040650161021
619097BV00014B/524